The United States

Missouri

Anne Welsbacher
ABDO & Daughters

visit us at
www.abdopub.com

Published by Abdo & Daughters, 4940 Viking Drive, Suite 622, Edina, Minnesota 55435.
Copyright © 1998 by Abdo Consulting Group, Inc., Pentagon Tower, P.O. Box 36036, Minneapolis, Minnesota 55435 USA. International copyrights reserved in all countries. No part of this book may be reproduced in any form without written permission from the publisher.

Printed in the United States.

Cover and Interior Photo credits: Super Stock, Peter Arnold, Inc., Corbis-Bettmann, Wide World

Edited by Lori Kinstad Pupeza
Contributing editor Brooke Henderson
Special thanks to our Checkerboard Kids–Francesca Tuminelly, Stephanie McKenna, Raymond Sherman

All statistics taken from the 1990 census; The Rand McNally Discovery Atlas of The United States. Other sources: *Missouri*, Fradin and Fradin, Children's Press, Chicago, 1994; *Missouri*, Sanford and Green, Children's Press, Chicago 1990; *Missouri*, LaDoux, Lerner Publications Co., Minneapolis, 1991; America Online, Compton's Living Encyclopedia, 1997; World Book Encyclopedia, 1990.

Library of Congress Cataloging-in-Publication Data

Welsbacher, Anne, 1955-
    Missouri / Anne Welsbacher.
    p. cm. -- (United States)
    Includes index.
    Summary: A brief overview of the geography, history, cities, and people of the Show-Me State.
    ISBN 1-56239-884-9
    1. Missouri--Juvenile literature. [1. Missouri.] I. Title. II. Series: United States (Series)
    F466.3.W45   1998
    977.8--dc21   97-18131
                                          CIP
                                          AC

Contents

Welcome to Missouri 4
Fast Facts About Missouri 6
Nature's Treasures 8
Beginnings 10
Happenings 12
Missouri's People 18
Missouri's Cities 20
Missouri's Land 22
Missouri at Play 24
Missouri at Work 26
Fun Facts 28
Glossary 30
Internet Sites 31
Index 32

Welcome to Missouri

Missouri is the front door to the West. The two longest rivers in the United States run through Missouri. Long ago, many railroads in Missouri carried people into the wild west. Two famous **pioneer** trails, the Santa Fe Trail and the Oregon Trail, began in Missouri.

Many lakes and rivers run through Missouri. Some are in the pretty Ozark Mountains, where people from all over the country come to visit. Missouri also has farms and grasslands.

Missourians have the reputation of wanting to know all the facts before they decide something. For this reason, Missouri is called the Show-Me State.

Opposite page: Missouri has a very beautiful landscape.

Fast Facts

MISSOURI
Capital
Jefferson City (35,481 people)
Area
68,945 square miles
(178,567 sq km)
Population
5,137,804 people
Rank: 15th
Statehood
Aug. 10, 1821
(24th state admitted)
Principal rivers
Mississippi River
Missouri River
Highest point
Taum Sauk Mountain;
1,772 feet (540 m)
Largest City
Kansas City (435,146 people)
Motto
Salus populi suprema lex esto
(The welfare of the people shall be the supreme law)
Song
"Missouri Waltz"
Famous People
Thomas Hart Benton, George Washington Carver, Samuel Clemens (Mark Twain), Joseph Pulitzer, Harry S. Truman

State Flag

Hawthorn

Bluebird

Dogwood

About Missouri
The Show–Me State

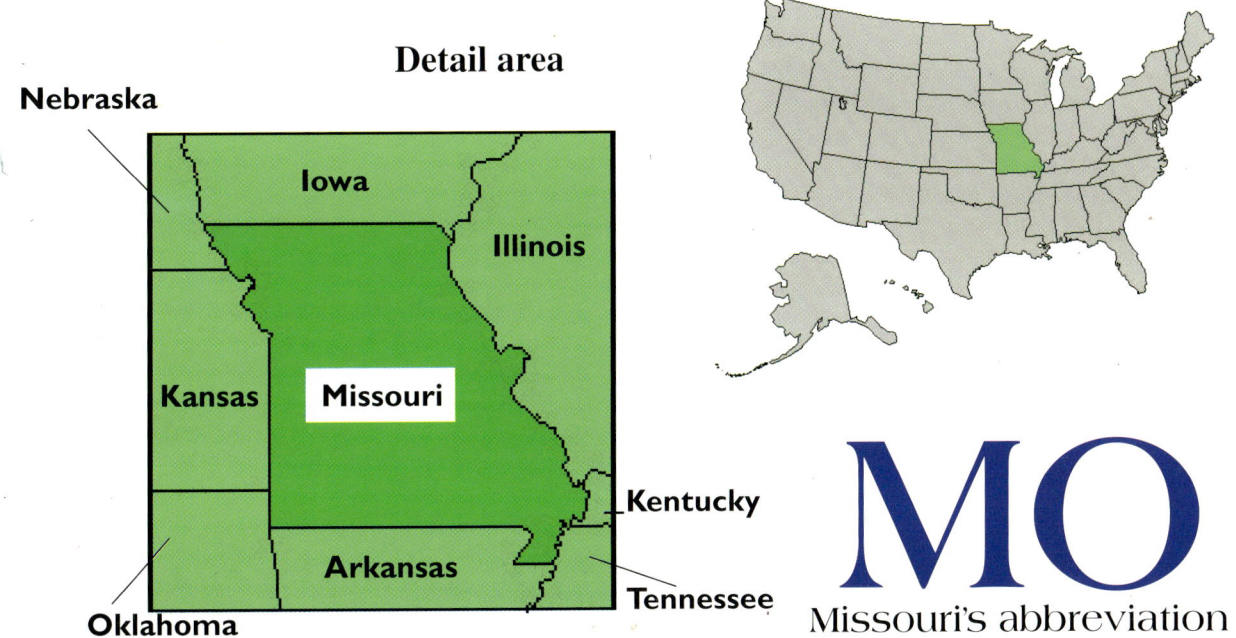

Borders: west (Nebraska, Kansas, Oklahoma), north (Iowa), east (Illinois, Kentucky, Tennessee), south (Arkansas)

Nature's Treasures

Missouri has many rivers, lakes, and springs. In the Ozark Mountains, warm water spurts up out of some of the springs! These **hot springs** are like hot tubs built by nature!

The water and the land have many minerals. They include lead, clay, iron, limestone, copper, and silver.

Missouri's weather is mild in the mountains. It can get hot in the lower lands. Much of Missouri also has rich soil that is good for farming.

*Opposite page:
The Missouri River.*

Beginnings

Native Americans came to Missouri about 10,000 years ago. Mound Builders came and built tall mounds.

In the late 1600s, Osage, Missouri, and Iowa people lived in Missouri. The Osage were six or seven feet (2 m) tall!

In the 1600s and 1700s, French fur trappers and settlers came to Missouri. In 1803, France sold Missouri and other areas to the United States. **Immigrants** moved to the United States. They pushed many Native Americans from the east into Missouri. Later they were pushed even farther southwest.

When Missouri wanted to be a state, people argued about whether or not it should allow slavery. They decided Missouri would have slaves and another new state called Maine would not allow slavery. This was called the Missouri Compromise. In 1821, Missouri became the 24th state.

In 1861, the Civil War began between the southern states and the northern states. Many southern states **seceded**.

Missouri did not secede. Many Missourians fought with the North. In 1865, when the Civil War ended, Missouri was the first slave state to free its slaves.

Because it was next to the long Mississippi River, St. Louis, Missouri, was the third largest city in the country in the late 1800s. Steamboats chugged down the river. Trains traveled east and west from St. Louis.

In 1904, a huge World's Fair was in St. Louis. It also was home to the world-wide Olympics in 1904. That year, the United States won every track and field event!

Civil War Scene

Happenings • Happenings • Happenings • Happenings • Happenings • Happenin

B.C. to 1803

Early Missourians

2000 B.C.-1500s: Mound Builders live in Missouri.

1600s: Osage, Missouri, and Iowa people move west into Missouri.

1700s: French fur trappers and settlers move into Missouri. Tribes are pushed further west from eastern United States.

1803: The French sell Missouri and other lands to the United States.

Happenings • Happenings • Happenings • Happenings • Happenings • Happenings

Missouri
B.C. to 1803

Happenings • Happenings • Happenings • Happenings • Happenings • Happenin

1821 to 1865

Early Statehood

1821: Missouri becomes the 24th state. The year before that the Misssouri Compromise says Missouri can have slavery.

1856-1860: Missourian **pro-slavers** battle with **abolitionists** in Kansas over the issue of slavery.

1865: The Civil War ends. Missouri is the first slave state to free its slaves.

Happenings • Happenings • Happenings • Happenings • Happenings • Happenings

Missouri

1821 to 1865

Happenings • Happenings • Happenings • Happenings • Happenings • Happenings

Late 1800s to Present

Big River, Big Cities

Late 1800s: Steamboats carry goods down the Mississippi River. St. Louis and Kansas City are big business towns.

1904: The World's Fair is held in St. Louis. It is the biggest World's Fair in history to that date. Many new machines are shown at the fair.

1945: Missourian Harry S. Truman becomes president of the United States.

1993: The Mississippi and other rivers in Missouri flood the whole state.

Missouri
Late 1800s to Present

Missouri's People

There are about 5.1 million people living in Missouri. Most live in cities. Some live in **rural** areas.

Many Missourians are white. One out of every 10 people in Missouri is African American.

Wild west rider Calamity Jane and outlaw Jesse James were born in Missouri. Baseball players Yogi Berra and Casey Stengel also were from Missouri. Berra played for the New York Yankees. Stengel played for many different teams, but became a legend managing the Yankees to seven World Series Championships.

Chuck Berry, the father of rock and roll music, was born in St. Louis. The writer Mark Twain, who wrote many books about the Mississippi River, was from Missouri. Poets Langston Hughes, T.S. Eliot, and Marianne Moore also were from Missouri.

The famous news reporter Walter Cronkite was born in St. Joseph, Missouri. The movie actor and director John Huston was born in Nevada, Missouri. Former United States president Harry Truman was born in Missouri. And civil rights leader Roy Wilkins was from St. Louis. He fought for equal rights.

Chuck Berry

Calamity Jane

Mark Twain

Missouri's Cities

Missouri has two big cities on each side of the state. The largest is Kansas City, on the west side. The next largest is St. Louis, on the east side.

Kansas City is famous for jazz music. It is also known for its barbecued ribs and other good food. St. Louis is next to the Mississippi River. A tall, wide arch over the river welcomes visitors to the city.

The capital of Missouri is Jefferson City. It is near the middle of the state. Independence, Missouri, was the home of Harry Truman. Springfield is in the pretty Ozark Mountains.

The famous St. Louis Arch in St. Louis, Missouri.

Missouri's Land

Missouri is shaped like a puzzle piece. The bottom, top, and west side are straight. The east side and three corners are crooked.

The northern part of Missouri is flat. Its rich soil is good for growing corn. In the bottom part of the state are rivers, valleys, and mountains. The Ozark Mountains are in this area.

The two longest rivers in the United States run through Missouri. The Mississippi River runs north to south along the eastern **border**. The Missouri River cuts through the state from west to east.

Missouri also has many caves. And it has fresh water springs under the ground! One of the largest caves has 200 miles of tunnels running through it!

Forests cover the lower part of Missouri. Growing in them are oak, hickory, and cottonwood. Flowers and plants like roses, violets, mint, and mistletoe grow wild in Missouri.

Deer, beavers, cottontail rabbits, skunks, foxes, and raccoons live in Missouri. Blue jays, woodpeckers, and quail are some of its birds. Bass, catfish, and trout swim in the lakes and rivers of Missouri.

Fog rolls in on the Missouri River.

Missouri at Play

Missourians have lots of ball teams to cheer! The St. Louis Cardinals and the Kansas City Royals both play baseball in Missouri. The Kansas City Chiefs, and the St. Louis Rams play football there. And the St. Louis Blues is a Missouri hockey team.

There are many parks, woods, and lakes to visit in Missouri. Meramec Caverns is where Jesse James hid from the law. There is a cave there large enough to hold 300 cars!

Kansas City and St. Louis have many music festivals. A famous symphony plays in St. Louis. Branson, Missouri, is home to country and western music.

Opposite page: Willie McGee goes to bat for the St. Louis Cardinals.

Missouri at Work

Most Missourians work in service. They sell cars and machines for farms, work in sports or health care, or work with railroads and river barges.

Kansas City and St. Louis have many good places to eat. So Missourians also work in the food business. They make cheese and butter. In St. Louis, many Missourians brew beer. In Kansas City, they mill flour.

Missourians make car parts, railroad cars, trucks, paint, soap, and other things. Some Missourians grow soybeans and corn and raise cows for beef.

Missouri is famous for news reporting, which is called **journalism**. The first **college** journalism school opened in Columbia, Missouri, in 1908. A college is a school you can go to after high school. Some Missourians work in journalism or at one of the state's colleges.

Feeding time at a Missouri cattle farm.

Fun Facts

- Ice cream cones were sold for the first time at the St. Louis World's Fair in 1904. A man selling ice cream was next to a man selling waffles. He put a waffle around some ice cream. The ice cream cone was **invented**!
- The first **parachute** jump from an airplane was made in Missouri. Captain Albert Berry made the jump near St. Louis in 1912.
- The Mark Twain Cave, near Hannibal, is the cave that Mark Twain used in his book *The Adventures of Tom Sawyer*. In the story, Tom and Becky Thatcher get lost in the cave. Mark Twain found the cave when he was still a boy.
- The first public school kindergarten opened in Missouri in 1873.
- More corncob pipes are made in Washington, Missouri, than in any other place in the world.

• The famous African-American scientist George Washington Carver was born in Missouri. He tried new things in a science that works with plants, called botany. Carver used farming to help African-Americans after the Civil War. He taught people to grow peanuts and sweet potatoes, not just cotton. This made their soil richer and helped grow more crops. Carver also invented more than 100 products dealing with the peanut.

The ice cream cone was invented in Missouri in 1904.

Glossary

Abolitionist: a person who did not want slavery during the time before the Civil War.
Border: the edge of something.
College: a school you can go to after high school.
Hot springs: springs of water under the ground that are heated by the earth; warm water comes out of the springs.
Immigrant: a person who comes from another country.
Invent: to make something for the first time.
Journalism: news reporting.
Parachute: a large balloon-like object that catches the air like a kite; people can wear a parachute to jump out of airplanes and land safely on the ground.
Pioneer: a person who goes somewhere for the first time.
Pro-slaver: a person who did want slavery during the time before the Civil War.
Rural: the country side, not the city.
Secede: to break away.
Union: a group.

Internet Sites

The Missouri Site of USGenWeb
http://www.rootsweb.com/~mogenweb/mo.htm
Come on in, make yourself at home, and look around for your kinfolks!

The 1864 Confederate Invasion of Missouri
http://www.geocities.com/CollegePark/Quad/6460/PrRd.html
Learn about Missouri's role in the Civil War. Learn about battles and different war heroes. Link to the battlefield web sites all in chronological order.

Gone But Not Forgotten'
Missouri Pioneers
http://www.rootsweb.com/~mopionee/
Missouri Pioneers is a group of settlers who settled in the state of Missouri by 1890. Many people send me their historical research and family histories. Please help this site continue to grow and submit your ancestors that settled in Missouri before 1890.

These sites are subject to change. Go to your favorite search engine and type in Missouri for more information.

PASS IT ON

Tell Others Something Special About Your State

To educate readers around the country, pass on interesting tips, places to see, history, and little unknown facts about the state you live in. We want to hear from you!

To get posted on ABDO & Daughters website E-mail us at "mystate@abdopub.com"

Index

A

abolitionists 10, 14
African American 18

C

caves 10, 22
cities 16, 18, 20
Civil War 11, 14, 29
college 26

F

farming 8, 29
farms 4, 26
flowers 23
French fur trappers 10, 12

H

hot springs 8

I

Immigrants 10

J

jazz music 20
Jefferson City 6, 20

K

Kansas City 6, 16, 20, 24, 26

L

lakes 4, 8, 23, 24

M

Meramec Caverns 24
Mississippi River 6, 11, 16, 18, 20, 22
Missouri Compromise 11
Missouri River 6, 22
Missouri's people 18
mound builders 10, 12
mountains 4, 8, 20, 22

N

Native Americans 10

O

olympics 11
Ozark Mountains 4, 8, 20

P

pioneer 4, 11

R

railroads 4, 26
rivers 4, 6, 8, 10, 16, 22, 23
rural areas 18

S

Santa Fe Trail 11
slavery 10, 14
sports 26
St. Louis 11, 16, 18, 19, 20, 24, 26, 28
steamboats 11, 16

T

Twain, Mark 6, 18, 28

W

weather 8
wild west 4, 18
World's Fair 11, 16, 28

DATE DUE			

977.8
WEL

3196039000450
Welsbacher, Anne.

Missouri

LONGFELLOW ELEMENTARY LIBRARY
HOUSTON, TX. 77025

399629 01495   42198C   014